My World of Science

CONDUCTORS AND INSULATORS

Angela Royston

Heinemann
LIBRARY

www.heinemann.co.uk/library
Visit our website to find out more information about **Heinemann Library** books.

To order:
☎ Phone 44 (0) 1865 888066
🖹 Send a fax to 44 (0) 1865 314091
💻 Visit the Heinemann Bookshop at www.heinemann.co.uk/library to browse our catalogue and order online.

First published in Great Britain by Heinemann Library, Halley Court, Jordan Hill, Oxford OX2 8EJ, part of Harcourt Education.

Heinemann is a registered trademark of Harcourt Education Ltd.

Editorial: Andrew Farrow and Dan Nunn
Design: Jo Hinton-Malivoire and
    Tinstar Design Limited (www.tinstar.co.uk)
Picture Research: Maria Joannou and Sally Smith
Production: Viv Hichens

Originated by Blenheim Colour Ltd
Printed and bound in China by
    South China Printing Company

ISBN 0 431 13726 9
07 06 05 04 03
10 9 8 7 6 5 4 3 2 1

**British Library Cataloguing
in Publication Data**
Royston, Angela
Conductors and insulators. – (My world of science)
1. Electric conductors – Juvenile literature
2. Electric insulators and insulation – Juvenile literature
I. Title
620.1'1297

A full catalogue record for this book is available from the British Library.

Acknowledgements
The publishers would like to thank the following for permission to reproduce photographs: Corbis (RF) p. **15**; Getty Images p. **17**; Network Photographers pp. **4**, **28**; Peter Gould p. **7** Photodisc pp. **6**, **29**; Science Photo Library/Custom Medical Stock p. **24**; Trevor Clifford pp. **5**, **8**, **9**, **10**, **12**, **13**, **14**, **16**, **18**, **19**, **20**, **21**, **22**, **23**; Trip pp. **11** (G. Hopkinson), **26** (H. Rogers), **25** (N. Price); Tudor Photography p. **27**.

Cover photograph reproduced with permission of Photodisc.

Every effort has been made to contact copyright holders of any material reproduced in this book. Any omissions will be rectified in subsequent printings if notice is given to the publishers.

Contents

Any words appearing in the text in bold, **like this**,
are explained in the Glossary.

What is a conductor?

A conductor allows heat or electricity to pass through it. This metal spoon gets hot because heat from the tea passes along it.

An electric wire conducts electricity. Electricity passes along the wire from the plug in the wall to the **motor** in the hairdryer.

What is an insulator?

An insulator does not allow heat or electricity to pass through it. The handle of this wooden spoon does not get hot, because heat cannot pass along it.

Wood and plastic are good insulators. Each of these wires is covered with plastic. Electricity from the electric wire cannot pass through the plastic.

What is electricity?

Electricity is a force that is used to make things happen. Electricity makes the toaster hot. When the toast is ready, it pops up.

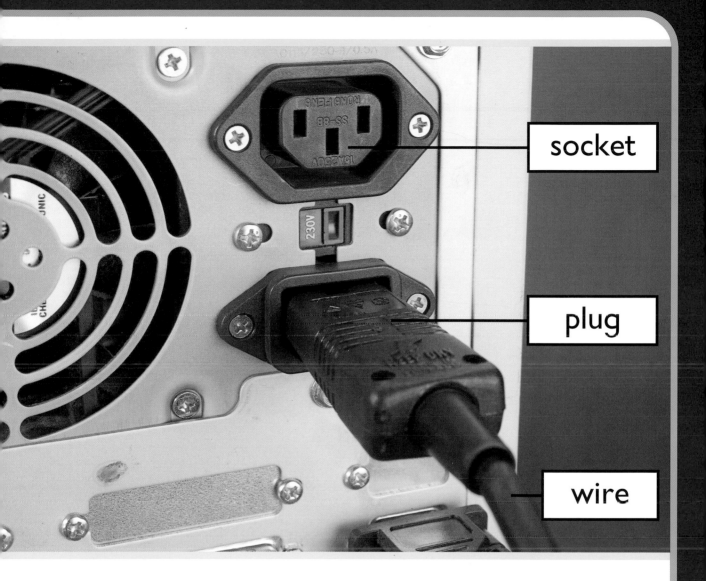

socket

plug

wire

Be safe! Do not touch bare electrical wires or electrical machines that may be hot. Never poke anything into an electric **socket** or electrical machine.

Conducting electricity

An electrical wire is made of thin strands of metal. The wire allows electricity to pass from the plug in the wall into the television and then back to the plug.

This train has an **engine** that runs on electricity. The electricity is conducted into the engine from the wire above the train.

A simple circuit

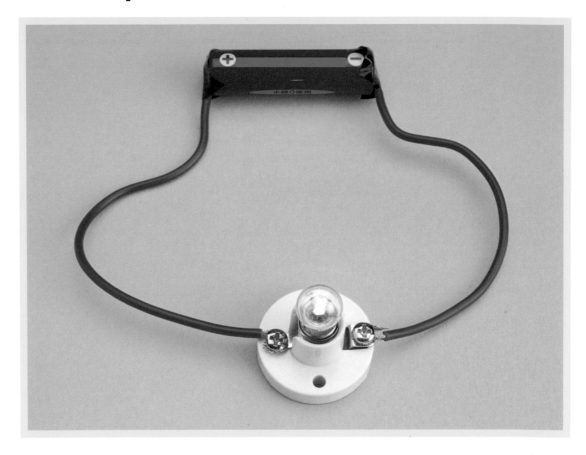

This is a simple **circuit**. The battery makes electricity. Wires conduct electricity from the battery to the bulb and back to the battery. The electricity lights the bulb.

Electricity will not flow if there is a gap in the circuit. Electricity cannot flow around this circuit. This is because there is a gap between the wire and the battery.

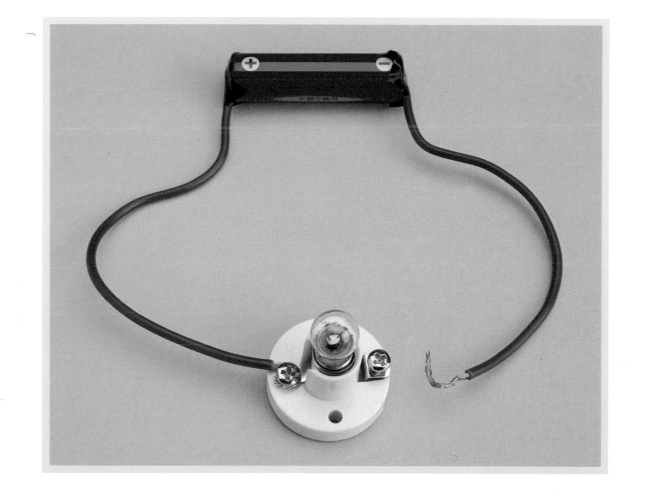

Water and electricity

Do not touch an electrical machine or an electric switch with wet hands. The water can conduct the electricity into your body and give you an **electric shock**!

Never put electrical machines in
water. This swimming pool has lights
under the water, but they are safe.
They have been specially sealed so
that the water cannot reach them.

Comparing metals

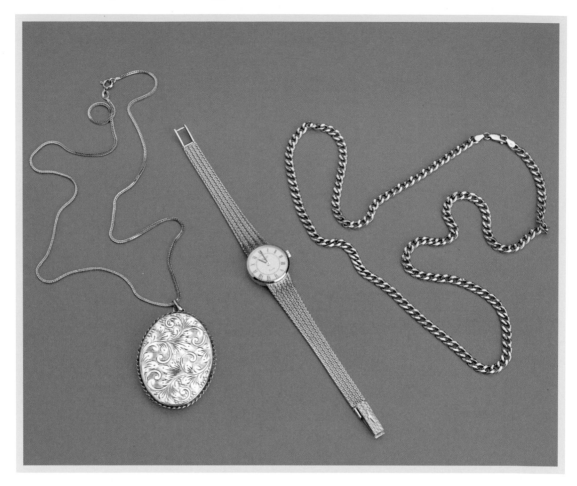

Some metals conduct electricity
better than other metals. **Gold** is
the best conductor of electricity,
but gold is very expensive.

Electric wires and cables are usually made of **copper**. Copper is a good conductor of electricity. It is also much cheaper than gold.

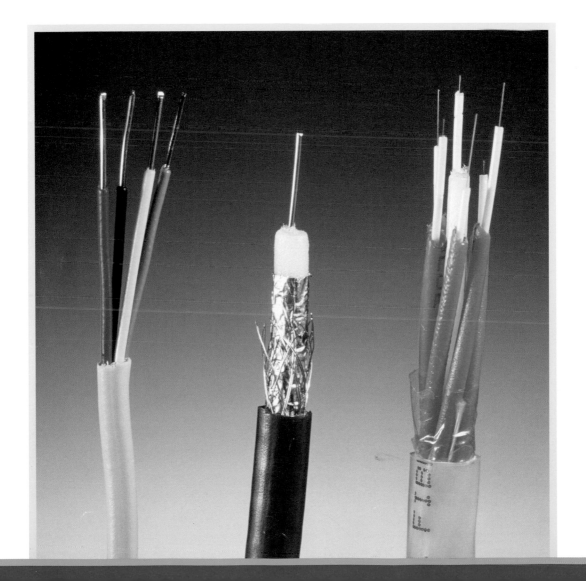

Conducting heat

Most metals conduct heat well.
When you touch metal things in
summer, the metal feels warm.
This is because heat flows from
the metal into your skin.

This pan has a layer of **copper** on the bottom. Copper is a good conductor. It quickly spreads heat across the bottom of the pan.

Good insulators

This boy is testing different materials to see whether they are good insulators. When he puts an insulator in the **circuit** the bulb does not light.

Rubber, cloth, plastic and wood are good insulators. Now he tests a leaf in the circuit. Is the leaf a conductor or an insulator? (Answer on page 31.)

Insulating air

Air can be a good insulator. An electric **circuit** must be complete before electricity can flow. Electricity cannot pass through the air from the battery to the torch.

A thermos flask has one **container** inside another. There is a space between them. The space insulates the inner container and stops heat escaping from it.

Clothes

Clothes are good insulators. This woollen jersey and blanket keep the woman warm. They trap warm air near her body.

The **fleecy** linings of these coats also trap warm air. The children's hats trap air too. What is keeping their hands warm? (Answer on page 31.)

Other insulators

Wool, cloth and thick paper do not allow heat to pass through them easily. This teapot is covered with a thick woolly **tea cosy** to keep the heat in.

This **takeaway** coffee is packed in a special cup that keeps the drink warm. The cup is made of **polystyrene**. Polystyrene is a good insulator.

Using conductors and insulators together

The metal plate under an **iron** gets very hot. The metal plate conducts the heat onto the clothes. The plastic handle insulates the person's hand from the heat.

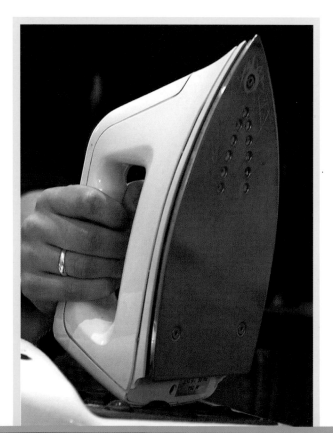

This person is taking a hot dish from
an oven. She uses oven gloves to
insulate her hands so they do not
get burnt. What are the oven gloves
made of? (Answer on page 31.)

Glossary

circuit path that allows electricity to flow around it

container object used to hold something

copper a kind of metal

electric shock a violent jolt that happens when electricity flows through the body. A powerful electric shock can kill you.

engine machine that makes something move

fleecy warm, light and fluffy

gold a kind of metal that costs a lot of money

iron a small heavy machine that uses heat to make clothes smooth

motor engine that uses electricity

polystyrene a kind of plastic that is light and airy

socket hole that an electric plug fits into. The socket joins the plug to electrical wires in the wall.

takeaway food and drink that you buy in a restaurant to eat and drink at home

tea cosy special cover used to keep a teapot warm

Answers

page 21
The bulb has not lit up. This shows that the leaf is an insulator.

page 25
Gloves are keeping the children's hands warm.

page 29
The oven gloves are made of thick cloth.

Index

Titles in the *My World of Science* series include:

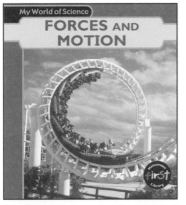

My World of Science
FORCES AND MOTION

Hardback   0 431 13700 5

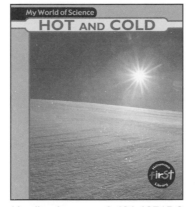

My World of Science
HOT AND COLD

Hardback   0 431 13715 3

My World of Science
LIGHT AND DARK

Hardback   0 431 13712 9

My World of Science
MAGNETS

Hardback   0 431 13704 8

My World of Science
MATERIALS

Hardback   0 431 13701 3

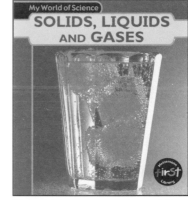

My World of Science
SOLIDS, LIQUIDS AND GASES

Hardback   0 431 13702 1

My World of Science
SOUND AND HEARING

Hardback   0 431 13714 5

My World of Science
USING ELECTRICITY

Hardback   0 431 13716 1

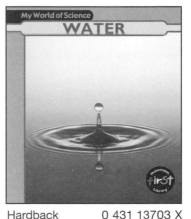

My World of Science
WATER

Hardback   0 431 13703 X

Find out about the other titles in this series on our website www.heinemann.co.uk/library